A poem is like a BELL ringing Crystal Clear in the head and heart.

All these original droplets of love jotted down by the hand of Crystal Bell will ring a BELL of JOY into your life.

This has been a lifetime of collecting and writing, all arranged in this book to bless your spirit and give you a new lift each day. I like to read one after devotions... like putting the cherry on the milkshake...just what I needed for that moment.

Thanks CRYSTAL BELL for ringing our bells... crystal clear...

Dr. Lonnie Rex
President, World Wide Compassion

WE WERE MADE TO
SHINE

WORDS *of* HEALING & CHANGE

CRYSTAL BELL

WE WERE MADE TO
SHINE

WORDS *of* HEALING & CHANGE

TATE PUBLISHING
AND ENTERPRISES, LLC

Published by Tate Publishing & Enterprises, LLC
127 E. Trade Center Terrace | Mustang, Oklahoma 73064 USA
1.888.361.9473 | www.tatepublishing.com

Tate Publishing is committed to excellence in the publishing industry. The company reflects the philosophy established by the founders, based on Psalm 68:11,
"The Lord gave the word and great was the company of those who published it."

Book design copyright © 2013 by Tate Publishing, LLC. All rights reserved.
Cover design by Rtor Maghuyop
Interior design by Jimmy Sevilleno

Published in the United States of America

ISBN: 978-1-62854-419-0
1. Poetry / Subjects & Themes / Inspirational & Religious
2. Poetry / General
13.11.05

Dedication

To my Heavenly Father first and foremost and then to my precious husband Monty (Beaver Bell), my brothers, children, grandchildren, nieces and nephews, friends, and all people who want to be free of the enemy and walk more closely with God.

Acknowledgments

Thank you to Dr. Lonnie Rex, for believing in me and for your help in getting this book published; my faithful husband, for always showing me God's love and support; and my mom and dad, now in heaven, for all they taught me about the Lord and how to look past myself and see the needs and hurts of other people. Thank you to my late pastor, Brother George Dustin, now in heaven, for all he taught me and showed me through his living the Word of God. I thank Brother Jabbo Green, for beginning my knowledge of the Word and the Holy Spirit.

Table of Contents

Dedication 7

Acknowledgments 9

Preface 17

Introduction 19

All They Need Is You 22

You're Always There 23

A Prayer for Life's Path 24

Love Is a Seed 25

To My Family 26

Willing to Learn 27

My Great Savior 28

The Answer 29

To the People of the World 30

Do You Know the One?. 31

A Burdened Heart 32

The Spirit of Life 33

Stubborn and Set 34

Some Think They Are Saved 35

A Special Love 36

Tarry Not 37

To My Heart 38
Examine Yourself 39
Thou Art Mine 40
Your Choice 41
Get Ready! 42
I Sent My Son 43
A Picture of True Suffering 44
Inner Beauty 46
Look Unto Me 47
There Is a Place 48
Your Precious Touch 49
Take a Look 50
I'm Yours Lord 51
My Mama 52
A Gift to You 53
A Life without Regret 54
My Most Beautiful Treasure 55
Dustin and Aaron 57
Why Not Try This? 58
The Lord's Rest 60
Which Choice Will You Make? 62
So You Call Yourself a Christian? 63
What's The Most Important Thing? 65
Have You Been Abused? 66
God Turns Evil for Your Good 68
Mighty and Great 69

Hard Times 70
The Greatest Love! 71
Physical or Spiritual Adultery 73
The Storms of Life 74
Working to Get There 76
Death. 77
Do Not Fear 78
My Heart's Desire 79
Grief 80
My Mom and I 81
Getting Through the Death
    of My Mom and Dad 82
When You Are Hurting. 84
God's Precious Light 85
How Effective Do You Want to Be? . . . 86
Do You Still Have a Conscience?. 87
Your Words 88
God Loves You 89
Do You Want Revival? 90
Don't Withhold from God 91
Michael and Jackie 92
Do You Care About Your Friends 94
What Is Wrong? 96
Let Me See You as You Are 97
Show Me 98
To My Mate 99

Tragedy and Relief 100
No Time to Waste 101
Are There Idols in Your Life? 102
To You Who Will Stand 104
Empty Me Lord 106
Teach Me to Teach My Children Lord . . . 107
You Are My Everything. 108
Time with You. 109
A Love That Will Never End! 110
You Lord Are the Utmost within My Soul . . 111
Teach and Change Me Lord. 112
Thank You Father for Sharing Mom
    and Dad with Us 114
To Know You More 116
Your Vessels 117
You Are the Key 118
Fully Consume Me Lord 119
The Greater You Love, the Greater the Pain . . 120
Rescue Me Lord 121
My Life Is Not Mine to Take 123
Thankfulness 124
Just a Vessel 125
I Want You to Be My Heart 126
So Much Keeps Happening 127
Where Did You Go, Lord? 129
I Must Have More!. 130

No Death Dwelleth Here 132
Only in Him 133
God's Fullness—Not Parts and Pieces . . . 134
Hidden Rejection 136
Do You Believe? 138
What Is Hindering Me from Happiness? . . . 140
Please Help Me Lord 143
A Deceiving Thought 145
Help Us to Understand 147
Press On 148
Raise Your People Up 149
Pain in the Sea of Life 150
You Justify Me 151
Let's Get Back to the Spirit and Power . . . 152
Don't Seek Your Own Need 154
America and God 155
Deliver Your People Lord 157
Possess Me Lord 159
Thank You for the Fires 160
Death and Resurrection 161
The Altar 162
Focus 164
Choose to Die to Self 166
Pain or Freedom? 168
Reveal the Hidden Desires 170
Help Me Lord 171

A Great Privilege 172

I'm Free 174

Consumed 176

I'm Going Through. 177

Only When 178

The Spirit of Truth and the Spirit of Deception . 180

Saved but...Don't Want

   to Hear It, Walk it, or Talk It 181

A Stronghold of Heaviness Is Broken. . . . 183

Why Is My Life Draining Out? 185

The Seed and Root of a Thought 188

Don't Let Deception Steal Your Faith . . . 191

Our Nation Is Covered 193

Let Me Become One with You Lord 194

Never Alone 195

Rest in His Timing. 197

I Gave All—What Will You Do? 198

Help People Understand the Way 200

No Good-byes 202

Afterword. 204

Preface

The Lord has given me poems since about 1984. They are a part of my life. They always seemed to flow out of my heart, and during the very hard times, the Lord would give me answers to the problem, sort of like a psalm in the Bible. They are anointed of God, and they have helped many people experiencing similar things, and I thank the Lord for continuing to use them as He wills. He has many tools to reach, touch and heal people. I thank Him for this tool. Ask Him to help you to see the enemy's schemes and devices that might be causing the issues you are facing or dealing with. Remember when He said, on the cross, "It is finished." This meant that He paid the full price for us to be completely whole in every area of our life—physically, spiritually, financially and mentally. If you are not walking in that place or heading in that direction, then the enemy has you bound in some way. Seek God and ask Him what it is, and He will show you. He paid for you to be whole (nothing broken and nothing missing). So please don't stay bound when He has made a way for you to be free. May the Lord open the eyes of everyone who reads this book to see how the enemy works in our lives using the deception and lies through his demonic spirits to entangle us and to bring us to the point of frustration, confusion, depression, despair, lethargy (or not being of any use to the kingdom of God), then for some death. I ask You, Father, in Jesus's name, to lose the person reading this book and to fill them to the full with Your Holy Spirit and do a complete and thorough work in them. Thank you for perfecting that which concerns each individual soul as they read and seek you Father. Show each one their destiny and help them to fulfill it in the name of Jesus. Amen. Thank you, Father.

Introduction

f you have just accepted Jesus as your Lord and Savoir or you did it years ago, the Lord loves us so much that He can't leave us bound up as we are. He paid the price for you to be totally free, and so He goes through layer by layer inside of us and shows us every weight that hinders us so we can know what to pray for and deal with to walk in His freedom. Sometimes we misunderstand what is happening when He starts dealing with us and shows us what needs to be changed.

Some run: They don't like what they see inside themselves, so they stay busy doing everything possible to keep from thinking about it, which doesn't fix the problem or get you free from it. As a matter of fact, it only gets worse, and the roots grow down even deeper into your soul (your mind, will, and emotions.) Let Him help you to be free of the heaviness and the torment.

Some give up: They think, "Great, here's something else. I just can't do this. Every time I turn around, it's something else." They are so tired of being tormented by the enemy that they teeter on the border of giving up. People don't understand that the enemy is the cause, whether it is generational curses from the sins of our forefathers and mothers or something we did that gave the enemy ground in us. No matter the cause, we must never give up. Ask God to send you help and knowledge to understand. Hosea 4:6 says that God's people are destroyed for lack of knowledge. We must ask for it. There have been times when the enemy was telling me to give up, but each time I would think, "What is there to go back to without God?" Then I would think of how horrible hell will be if I give up—with being in constant hunger, thirst, torment, total darkness, separation from all my loved ones and God for all eternity. Just thinking about it gives me a boost to keep on walking through the trials. There is nothing on this earth, including not forgiving someone, that is worth missing heaven over. That always helps me get past that thought.

Some cover up: They are shown something that God wants them to deal with inside their selves, and they think they can't handle it. Then the enemy comes and tells them that it's okay and God shouldn't be asking so much from you and here, just take these pretty little pills, and here is a nice big bottle to help you drown and wash away all that nasty stuff that God was trying to get you to see. The only problem is it's all still there when they wake up the next day, plus whatever side effects, and the devil still has them bound and miserable. If you will ask God for His strength, you won't fall so much as when you depend on your own strength.

In each case, they don't realize that God is loving them by exposing what the enemy is doing in them to bring them out of all the bondage to freedom and true happiness. As He shows us something, we must ask His help and knowledge to get free of it. He loves us far past any problem we might have. Remember that He called us to be His child even when we were living in sin so He will not ever leave us while we are working through issues to be free, no matter how bad we think they are. He paid for all in full. So choose Jesus and life today; He will not reject you. He will be with you when there is no one else. He is faithful!

All They Need Is You

Oh gracious Lord above
Please send down your winds of love
To touch each and every heart
So that they may have a brand-new start
Maybe then they will see
How to love both you and me
Then what happiness they would feel
Instead of wanting only to kill
If the people only knew
All they really need is You

You're Always There

My problems lay so heavy on my mind
And leave me in a very big bind
Please Jesus help me out
And get my heart up and about
You are the only one to help me I know
Even though it doesn't always show
I know I will feel better in the mornings first light
Because you always make everything all right
Thank You Jesus for being there
I know that you will always care

A Prayer for Life's Path

I pray God is with you each second of your life
To help you through all the troubles and strife
His eyes watch every step you take
No matter what mistakes you might make
His heart fills yours with compassion and love
So one day you can see the Lord above
His hands pick you up when you fall
So you can once again stand straight and tall
His feet carry you when times are bad
And helps you when you are lonely and sad
His love shelter you from the wrong
So your life will be prosperous and long

Love Is a Seed

My heart is filled with profound love
For my Savior Lord above
He loves everyone you see
And is always there for you and me
Glory will you always know
If for the Lord you do sow
All you do is plant a seed
And He will meet your every need
Love people in your heart
And help them to make a start
Praise the Lord for what you've got
Though it might not be a lot
Look around and you will find
Others in a greater bind

To My Family

To a special man who has worked hard all of his life
To make a living for his kids and his wife
To a fine lady who keeps us all together
Through any type of difficult weather
To my first brother who always stands behind me
No matter what size my problems might be
To my second brother who is sentimental at times
And gives to me cards with beautiful rhymes
To these four kind people who are set apart
Your memories are eternally engraved into my heart
It doesn't matter what you might do
I will always be thankful for a family like you

With an everlasting love,
Crystal

Willing to Learn

My dear sweet Savior how I love thee
No matter what my problems might be
Please take me my Jesus and make me whole
It will bring me so much closer to my goal
My heart is ready and willing to learn
For I am overly eager for my turn
Praises to you Jesus I will always give
For through you I know I will always live

My Great Savior

All my sorrows and burdens to Him I give
And for my great Savior it is that I live
I am here my Father to carry out your will
I know you are with me as I go over each hill
You are my strength when I am weak
You are my everything that I seek
Praises to You Jesus I shall inevitably render
For You and Your righteousness I stand a defender

The Answer

A young man almost twenty
Problems yes plenty
In his head they rumble
All in a huge jumble
Confusion it seems has taken its toll
And now has everything out of control
Look up my son I am here
For I will take away the fear
Seek for me and you will find
The answer to clear up your mind
With me you have eternal life
With the world you have only strife

To the People of the World

Oh people of the world why must you be so blind
You've wrapped yourself in darkness
and bottled up your mind
The world is filled with stench of the evils that are done
And still Satan wants you each and every one
It's not too late yet if you want to change your path
So you won't be falling under God's terrible wrath
But if you choose to follow along with the worldly way
There's only one thing more that I really have to say
Soon God will return and it will be too late
For you to burn with Satan this will be your fate

Do You Know the One?

Do you know the one in whom I do confide?
Do you know the one who dwells with me inside?
Do you know of His mercy that He shows to mankind?
Do you know of His great love that
you only need seek to find?
His name is Jesus the God of my salvation!
The intercessor between God and every nation
He gave His life so that I could live
To Him praise and worship will I always give

A Burdened Heart

Millions of people I always see
But where are they to spend their eternity?
So many are still blind and lost
Yet they don't know of their great cost
As each new day comes and goes by
I sit with my head in my hands and cry
One by one I see them on judgment day
"I called you but you would not come," the Lord will say
"You turned away, so what else is there to do"
"From this day on I also will turn my face from you"
As I saw the lost cast into hell
Again my heart broke as some weak shell
If only they would let go of the ego,
stubbornness and pride
They could receive wisdom and knowledge
that the Lord will so willingly provide
Oh people, do you not see
Your life here is but a short time to be
Eternity is where all other time will be spent
Is it heaven or hell your soul will be sent?

The Spirit of Life

Praise God, I am a new creature
The new man is now my main feature
The Lord has given me His gift of the Holy Ghost
There is nothing else in this world that I treasure the most
I thank God each day for opening my eyes
To His precious Word, He is now making me wise
Now, " with God," do I pray
Instead of only me having my say
His Spirit has given me eternal life
Above and beyond all troubles and strife
So as my life here on earth shall come to an end
To my Lord, the Spirit and I shall then ascend

Stubborn and Set

To you who are stubborn and set in your ways
Just think of all the wasted time and days
You are so certain and sure of yourself
When it comes to God's Word there on your shelf
Ready in a heartbeat to argue or fight
For no one knows The Word as you do, in your sight
In your sight you think you know it all
But in God's sight you are as bitter as gall
Right here is the key you need my friend
To put your uneasiness to its end
To go on your sight of things would be absurd
You must go on God's sight of His Holy Word
You only need to ask with a seeking heart
And He will more than graciously do His part
Just open up your heart to Him and you will learn
And to your stubborn ways you will not return

Some Think They Are Saved

Lord why do some think that they are saved
But do not walk the road that you have paved?
Their attitude and ways are still the same
They don't depend on the One whom overcame
They act mean and nasty and do not care
They snap at you when the Lord you share
They quote the scriptures and use them against you
While all along they don't believe them to be true
My child, they have been deceived
and think that they are right
They do not keep the word as a mirror in their sight
The key to know if you are right will always be my love
If you don't then your walk is not from above
Many that had that love has now let it grow cold
Some go through the motions but it is of old
They need fresh fire that only I can give
I want fullness for them so they can fully live

A Special Love

My precious Lord I hope and pray
Your love within me grows each day
I desire to walk in your mighty love
As strong as a bear and as gently as a dove
Your love is faithful and shall not be rendered
Your love knows no time and will not be hindered
I want to love people as you do
No matter what they might have gone through
Reach through me with your love and touch
Each precious soul that you love so much

Tarry Not

My little lamb, you are so precious to me
Please listen, I want you to see
With each and every beat of your heart
Know this that I shall never depart
Why do you hold onto the burdens
that tear your heart in two?
Give them to me, the One who has
already worked them through
For you have no time to be weighted down
I have lost sheep that must be found
So tarry not before the gate
Or for some it will be too late

To My Heart

I speak to you heart have no fear
For the King of kings is standing near
You must be steadfast and do not give
For it is eternal life you want to live
You must trust in the Lord up above
Then you'll be secure in His sweet love
Then heart you will never be shaken
And from the Lord you'll never be taken

Examine Yourself

My little children can you not see
The true reason I have called you to me?
Yes, in victory you have learned to walk
And in My love you have now learned to talk
Being filled with many blessings you now have grown fat
And do not have the same zeal as where you were once at
There should be an extreme urgency
in your heart to win the lost
For I have paid the complete price
and it was the highest cost
Examine yourself there is much work to be done
And I'll replace the fire for the souls that must be won

Thou Art Mine

You dare to steal from me what I own
I spared no expense the price is shown
As I look at the life from me you have taken
I see it has been broken and badly shaken
How much more is your life able to endure?
Return it to me for I am the cure
The enemy has cunningly deceived you so
And does not want to let you go
So look to me before time runs out
I am the only way without one doubt

Isaiah 43:1 (KJV)

Your Choice

People come and people go
Some are willing and some say no
You set your path by the choice you make
Heaven or hell, which will you take?
There is no gray, it's black or white
Which do you live, wrong or right?
You can't speak God's Word and not live it too
Or heaven's gates will not be opened for you

Get Ready!

Christ is coming soon, Get ready!
Is there no urgency, no panic, no fear? Get ready!
Signs of the end are at hand, Get ready!
Wars, rumors of war, famines and earthquakes, Get ready!
Lovers of pleasure more than lovers of God, Get ready!
Marrying and giving in marriage, Get ready!
Make your decision now, stand firm, Get ready!
Or will morning find you cold without
another chance? Get ready!

I Sent My Son

I sent My Son to shed His blood
That you might be washed in the cleansing flood
The highest price has been paid
The road for you is already laid
Is it such a sacrifice to live for me?
For I return to you much more than you can see

A Picture of True Suffering

As I think on all the sorrow and pain that
seems to have ripped my heart in shreds
At times my whole being seems to be
hanging by only mere threads
I try so hard sometimes to understand
and figure things out
But all this seems to do is to bring more stress about
I thought maybe it would help to
talk to other people about it
But this only opened up the wounds; the anger and the
hurt that would not quit
Then one night as I was praying and
asking God's will to be done
He showed me a brutal picture of the suffering of His Son
From nails driven deep in His flesh and
beatings ripping away His hide
To His body jolting in excruciating pain as the
cross was thrust into place and a spear
pierced His side

He suffered more by taking on the
sins of each and every soul
Than anything that I will "ever" experience or know
Please forgive me Lord for all my complaining
As longsuffering and humbleness I'll ever be attaining

Isa. 53:7, I Timothy 1:16,
I Peter 5:8–11 (Amplified)

Inner Beauty

We all know the stunning beauty of a rose
But soon will be wrinkled as everyone knows
The true beauty, the seed, lays hidden deep within
And soon will start life all over again
We all too often look upon the outward shell
And forget that the outward beauty will one day fail
We should look on the beauty that lies within
And that seed that will start life over again
Jesus is that precious seed
He springs up to meet your every need
His beauty will always shine through you
To touch any soul that you will speak to

John 12:24–26 (Amplified)

Look Unto Me

Oh my children, when will you learn
There is no one else to whom you can turn
Only I am able to take the pain
And turn it all around for your gain
It hurts me so to see you cry
With gut-wrenching pain deep in your eyes
If you will only reach out to me
I will be "everything" you need me to be
My love far exceeds your understanding
It gives healing and is not demanding
I loved you all when you were blind in sin
And yet that love unfolds as to me you come in

There Is a Place

There is a place I long to see
There is a place I soon shall be
A place where no sorrow shall enter in
A place where there's no scars of sin
My Father patiently awaits me there
Ready my happiness with me to share
Singing and dancing like never told
Glory to glory that will ever unfold
A place that's full of joy and love
And all my loved ones up above
That place you cannot enter in
If Jesus hasn't redeemed you from your sin
So please accept Him into your heart
So of this place you can be a part

Your Precious Touch

Jesus each precious touch is better than the touch before
And yet I cannot be satisfied I always want more
I always like to hear your sweet voice
So gentle and loving this is my choice
I never want you to leave my side
Continually preparing me as I abide
I want totally to please you so very much
And this only can I achieve through your loving touch

Take a Look

Are you the kind who readily points out peoples faults,
Quick to tell them that they need to bring them to a halt?
So willing to tell someone exactly what they need to do
Before it's too late and they're not able to make it through
Have you just once taken a look deep inside yourself,
And compared your actions to God's
Word there on your shelf?
Once you take a look at what your own heart contains
You won't be so quick to point out other people's stains
Instead, you'll have more mercy on those that you see
And you will want to pray for them that they'll be set free

I'm Yours Lord

My precious Lord, my heart is yours, all the way through
There is nothing that for you I would not do
Inside and out without a doubt
From my most inner being I shout
Whether my situation looks good or bad
Whether I feel happy or extremely sad
I can never live without You Father
My heart could never handle all the bother
I know there's a reason for the things that happen to me
You are molding and cutting me to fit your plan I see
I know you'll turn the bad things around for
my good as in Your Word it does say
So you can do a work, in and through me,
to help and touch the people each day
I give you all the praise for any goodness in me
Without you showing me what's
right I know I would not see
Use me Lord in whatever way you will choose
To turn hearts away from the path
that their souls they will lose

My Mama

You calm the storms
You shine through the night
So precious are my thoughts of you
You make everything all right
For there is no one that could ever fill your place
No matter what the situation
No matter what the case
You are a precious jewel so fine and so rare
I give praise to God for this blessed gift
Your beauty goes deep and is beyond compare
I just cannot imagine life without you
I love you my mother more deeply than time
But God's grace will lead me through

A Gift to You

A treasured gift I give to you
A seed, a baby, so fresh and new
With you I share this precious life so bright
This life I place within your care aright
How will you mold this little life?
Will it be peace or will it be strife?
Will you teach the babe from whence it came,
Or will you let others teach the slander of my name?
Will you tell of my great love,
Or will you teach push come to shove?
You set this little one on a path
Either to show love or to show wrath
You will have to stand and answer one day
For what you did or didn't say
It is not ever too late to start
Just ask me and I'll speak it to your heart
You do not want to see that life end so sadly
If you love the child correct it and it won't end badly

A Life without Regret

To the people of the world
Why must you be so blind?
You'd rather let the children go
Than paddle their behind
You do not set the boundaries
That they need so bad to learn
And so they run wildly
And get into everything with little or no concern
You do not teach them the importance
of submitting to authority
So they learn to run in rebellion
With a great lack in priority
Then when they grow up and have gotten
into trouble, time and time again
You then get angry and want to lock them up
Is this not in itself a sin
If you would teach them in the beginning
To respect and to love
Then they could live a life without regret
And one day see the Lord above

My Most Beautiful Treasure

I'm so very blessed beyond any measure
Buried down deep in my heart is a most beautiful treasure
My Father has carefully placed various jewels
with a brilliant diamond right in the middle
If you'll take a moment to think it's
not really that much of a riddle
You see Jesus is the diamond in the middle casting
His sparkling love upon each of the other Stones
My mom and dad are set next to Him, reaching through
them to touch the jewels He has given to them on loan
There are two little jewels that the
Lord has shared with me
I know will outshine many in the days that they will see
Then there are my loving brothers, through
whom the Lord has multiplied my jewels
and Blessings many times unspoken
Each of these stones is rare, irreplaceable
and specifically chosen
Each of these jewels is so very precious to me,

That the Lord has cushioned each one
with love, grace and His mercy
I try to be so careful not to scratch
or harm them in any way
So that they will shine so bright as they become the
diamond I know each one of them will be One day

To: Mom, Dad, Dustin, Aaron, Michael, Kim, Jackie,
Lelania, Brandon, Colby and Krystal, Candace,
Nolan and Cady, Will, Coty, Kaylan, Mason, Morgan,
Kaden, Robin, Brooke, Carter and now even more
blessed through my husband, Beaver Bell, and the
jewels of his children and grandchildren that he shares
and are precious to me: Amye and Cory, Rebecca, Jake,
Samantha, Zoe, Monty and Stephanie, Casey and Chloe

Dustin and Aaron

Always let your heart be honest and true
And you'll have many rewards when here
on earth your race is through
You are both so very special to me
God chose you out of all the other
little boys on earth, you see
I pray He plants your feet firmly in Himself to stand
So you will pass through everything
while holding to His hand
I thank God for blessing and prospering both of you
As with Him you travel the road of life
that you must walk through
I love you two boys with all of my heart
No matter what you do or when we're apart

> With my undying love,
> Mama

Why Not Try This?

Living for God my friend is not for the weak
The weak are those who choose "not" for God to seek
It takes great strength to choose what is right
And not take the way that appears
easy in this world's sight
The way that may look easy is not always the best
It's fun at first but at the end there's no rest
When is the last time that you felt at peace,
Instead of wanting your life to cease?
You say, "But it's no fun to live this way"
You've tried everything else, why not try this today?
What? Are you telling me you're too scared to try?
You're so quick to try anything else so please, don't be shy
A lot of the other things ended up so bad
And left you so lonely and very sad
This is an experience you'll never forget
Unlike some that left you feeling like a target
There is another thing I would like to say
You don't have to change one single thing about your way

God takes all of us just as we are
Because no one is quite perfect by far
If you come across some Christians who say you
must change before you give God your heart
Please forgive them; they are in great need
of your prayers on their own part

The Lord's Rest

Only "in You" Lord, do I know I can rest
No matter how simple or how hard the test
That place of rest is so hard to find
When I try to figure the answers out in my mind
But once I learn and choose to hand it over to you
I can now see that you have already worked it through
I'm so thankful for your patience with me Father
And that you don't see me as just a bother
Please help all of your children to find your rest
So they can go on to fulfill your will and have the best

For the next three poems, the Lord kept me up for two nights before my daddy died. Both nights He gave me a total of three poems. On the morning of July 21, 1995, my dad was feeling bad and hurting in his arm and chest. My mom and I tried to get him to go to the hospital, but he refused. So I said, "Dad, since you won't let me take you to a doctor, would you like to hear what the Lord gave me the last two nights?"

Dad said yes, and I read the poems to him. Exactly ten to fifteen minutes later, he went home to be with the Lord. I give my eternal thanks to my Lord and my Savior for His mercy and His abundant goodness!

Which Choice Will You Make?

The road that leads to heaven my
friend is very very narrow
But this doesn't mean you have to be stiff
and walk as straight as an arrow
Wide is the road that seems so good
and will lead you into hell
Once you die, that ends your choice, no
matter how much you scream or yell
All through your life God gives you
that special choice to make
He doesn't push, He leaves it up to you,
is it heaven or hell you'll take?
Don't get me wrong, it pierces God's heart
when you choose the way that is wrong
He already paid for you by His Son's blood
so by all rights "to Him" you belong

So You Call Yourself a Christian?

So you call yourself a Christian and
say you live a life that's right
But how many people have you condemned
and caused to run in fright
You point your finger at them and say, "What's
wrong with you don't you know"
You can't do this you can't look like
that or to hell you will go
So in your heart you feel so smug and
say, "I've done my good deed"
But all you've done is gone and spewed
poison all over that fresh new seed
Instead of lifting them up you've torn
them down right at the very start
Their brand-new heart God gave to
them you have now ripped apart
Just whose side are you on, you tell me my friend?
Is it God or Satan who has worked
through you at the very end?

Have you now wounded them and pushed them
farther away from God by what you've said or done?
If this is so, it is not for God, this battle that you have won
You must think first not to offend with
the things that you might say
So you won't have to answer for turning a soul toward hell
When you stand before the Lord one day
Let me say this one thing just to help you out
God will work in love and not condemn, if there is a doubt
He wants us to tell and show His
unconditional love to them
So He can do a thorough work and
restore them completely unto Him

What's The Most Important Thing?

The most important thing my friend
is the condition of your heart
Is yours clean or is it all clogged up
or maybe it's torn apart
You see it is your heart that the Lord looks at
And not whether you're dressed this way or that
The Lord knows your every thought and its
intent as in your heart they do abide
You see there is not one thing hidden in your
heart that from the Lord you can hide
So why not turn your heart over to the
one who knows it inside and out
And let Him love you and restore you and
replace all of the fear and doubt

Have You Been Abused?

Have you been abused by someone in your life
And had to live in constant pain fear and strife?
At first it rips your very being into pieces
And it seems as if the pain never ceases
No matter what you do you're always wrong
To the one who has hurt you all along
You pray so hard that your partner will change
To give you love instead of hits in exchange
No matter how much love you started out with for them
Eventually it grows cold, hard and very very dim
If you have children, manipulation
and control is their game
To hurt and cut you through your
children in the very same
It seems an unending cycle, that you'll never be free
While outsiders look on harshly because
they don't understand or see
There has been Christians used of the
enemy to tighten those chains

They say "God hates divorce" so just pray
and God will help with those pains
My friend God does hate divorce only
when He has put one together
But how many people ask God to bring
the one that will last forever?
God knows who it will work with and who it will not
So ask and wait on Him and He'll bring you to that spot
God doesn't want His children living in torment and strife
He wants us to live in peace and to have a prosperous life
He will bind up your wounds and heal your heart
So you can have a brand-new start
He loves you so very much my dear friend
And He wants to love and shelter you till the end

God Turns Evil for Your Good

What people mean for your harm God
will turn around for good
This is something that is seldom understood
Do you truly trust God for each day of your life,
Or do you deal with the confusion and strife?
He will lovingly place your footsteps each day
If you'll not fear and let God have His own way
To do this it takes a lot of trust you know
And trust only comes in a close relationship that you grow
Closeness only comes by spending time with someone
This is a daily walk with Jesus God's Son
Just as Joseph's brothers meant him great harm
God turned it around and made him Egypt's right arm
God will do no less in your situation
So look to Him in a crisis with great expectation

Mighty and Great

You are so mighty you are so great
There is not one thing you did not create
The depth of your love is an endless motion
Never to cease with your undying devotion
Your wisdom far exceeds what little we can try to retain
As with it you turn our mistakes around for our own gain
Your faithfulness is beyond that of any mother
Even when I mess up you are there like no other
Your forgiveness out loves any mistake I can make
This is an exceptional love that is for my own sake
So willing are you to see me through
I give you my life and my heart that is true

Hard Times

The hard times in our lives are for a special reason
It is preparing us for a particular time and season
Faith is like a muscle at any length
You must work a muscle to build its strength
Your spiritual muscle must grow strong
If you are going to stand against the wrong
God allows trials to try this muscle out
From these He knows we will become very stout
Eventually able to stand any test
And to be able to do it through God's rest
So when the next hard time comes along
Look to God for your strength and sing Him a song
You will be surprised what this will do
As through that trial you'll more easily pass through

The Greatest Love!

The greatest love that ever will be
Is the love of God I pray you will see
Would you give your life to save a soul by chance
Or maybe even a few in a bad circumstance?
Would you try more than once if they resisted you
Or would you say, "Oh well, your problem, I'm through?"
If they hurt you many times over
and said, "Sorry, forgive me"
Would you have mercy or say, "Tough,
that's your last chance buddy?"
Would you take pity and lead and
guide them without a doubt
Or would you say, "You got yourself
in it, now get yourself out"?
God sent His Son Jesus to die for all
To accept or reject Him is your call
He'll forgive you no matter how many times
Only if it's true repentance your heart chimes
He'll lead and guide you as long as you want Him too

He wants to help you all the way through
He knows you're not perfect so don't try to be
Just keep your heart right with Him and heaven you'll see

Physical or Spiritual Adultery

You know in your heart that it's wrong
But still you continue to sing your song
Your heart slowly becomes hardened to the sin
And your relationship with God is broken then
Trying to stay independent and free
You run from all rules and restraints you see
Whether physical or spiritual adultery you will deteriorate
Slowly but surely it is a horrible state
A sin that is gradual and very deceitful too
A pretty start but an ugly end as it turns and bites you
In search for happiness you've been so brave
To your own desires you've become a slave
An unending cycle you can't seem to change
Only God can restore and rearrange
No matter what you do God's love for you is great
He will reconcile, heal and elevate
If you'll turn to Him, He'll forgive you and open the door
He wants you to know Him like never before

The Storms of Life

Suffering, setbacks and hardships will occur
And sometimes leaves everything in a blur
A life doesn't last as long as it may seem
The older you get you know just what I mean
Whether you're a child of God or you've chosen not to be
The storms rage on without an eye to see
Those without God Sometimes end up with no hope
And so they turn to the liquor, the gangs or the dope
Storms don't care whose lives are in its path
As it destroys while it unleashes its ugly wrath
To a child of God no matter what
damage is done at the end
They know if they'll hold to His
hand, its victory He will send
No matter if the damage is great or small
God is able to turn it into good for us all
Some who will read this has chosen to go it alone
You say, "No, I don't see it, I've never been shown"

I dare you to just call out to Him
and try to prove me wrong
You see "I know" you'll walk away
singing a brand-new song

Working to Get There

There are some who work so hard to be saved
Not realizing the road has already been paved
They think by keeping certain customs
and traditions day and night
They will gain God's favor and make
them acceptable in His sight
Some think, "I've not hurt anyone,
actually, I'm kind of nice"
While others think with attending and giving
at church this will pay their price
No matter how sincere your efforts are my friend
You'll not find salvation for you at the end
Salvation is something you will never be able to earn
You get it, only by faith, but without it you'll burn
Trusting in Jesus will give you everything
you've been working to get
It will lift your burden and for eternal life you will be set

Death

From the moment you're born you start to die
A fact you can't change no matter what you try
So why fear death your whole life through
When God will share eternal life with you
If you'll just let Jesus into your heart to live
An abundant and eternal life to you He'll give
If you choose to reject Him and not let Him in
You will send your own soul to hell by this one sin
Remember you are not promised your next breath
You don't know when you'll meet up with death
So never put this off or it could be too late
Once you die that ends you choice
you've sealed your own soul's fate
If you're his child, to be absent from the body
is to be present with the Lord above
So we look forward to that day to go home and
to live with our family and Lord in love

Do Not Fear

Little one you have nothing to fear
I've walked the path before you and I am always near
I send grace and mercy along with you
And there is forgiveness for all that you do
There is a purpose for all that touches your life
Lessons to be learned but not to end in strife
If you give your heart to me
I'll keep you for all eternity
No one is able to take you from my hand
No one before me is able to withstand

My Heart's Desire

God, my soul hungers and thirsts for you
With a fervent desire for all that is true
Draw me closer to your precious side
I will ever with you abide
I yearn to love people the way you do
Even those that have wounded me all the way through
I crave to see people through your eyes
Not to judge or condemn them and act unwise
Under no condition do I want to miss what you say to me
I don't want to miss leading anyone into eternity
All that I am and have Father is yours to use
Change or rearrange it in any way that you choose
I am yours Lord in whatever your will
It's you who strengthens me and not by my own skill

Grief

Sometimes I feel I'm a prisoner of my own mind
It shoots thousands of thoughts at
me of the strangest kind
My mind don't even want with me to console
It's as if it is trying to take full control
Into my mind it ushers in a thick fog of confusion
Knowing this one tool will bring him
even closer to his solution
Quickly he orders heaviness in all around me
As he sends in depression, he hopes this will be the key
Faster and faster flies the thoughts through my head
It's too much! Then enters the
thought, "I wish I were dead"
The enemy uses grief like a door while you are weak
To wound you or to take your life he does always seek
You have the control over these thoughts in Jesus's Name
Just command them to go out the same way they came
Then thank and praise God for what He has done
It will make your race a little easier to be run

My Mom and I

We were woven together from the very start
With a bond only God can give inside a heart
You mama are like no other
God gave you to me as my sweet mother
God carefully made you especially for me
He knew you would love me like no one else you see
A blessed woman so tried and true
God put it all inside of you—
You are a part of all that I am and all that I will do
And I will eternally thank God for the gift of you
My heart will never beat the same
For there's an empty space that ever calls your name
The silence echoes back all the way to the beginning
With all kinds of thoughts which I now am penning
Without you mama my life will never be the same
Till my work here is through and it's heaven I claim

Getting Through the Death of My Mom and Dad

I know Lord, I truly do not wish them to be back
To have to bear upon themselves the
cares of this life to have to pack
I'm ever so thankful for you having taken them home
Now with exceeding joy, you and their
loved ones, they'll forever roam
But Father, I need your help so desperately bad
My heart feels mortally wounded, so broken and very sad
Something deep inside me is screaming in agony and pain
Like my world has fallen apart and
my mind is going insane
I know you have other things for me to do
Yet I can't think right to see a way through
Your Word says you bottle each tear that I cry
I used to always stop and wonder the reason why
That is an indescribable love for
someone, even in their pain

That their tears are so precious to you,
no matter what the strain
For each soul you have such an unfathomable love
So your pain for us must be as unexplainable as that above
I know on my own I can do nothing without you
I thank you for healing my heart and
showing me what I must do

When You Are Hurting

When you are hurting and when you are weak
When you can't even get your mind to think
If your world has been completely torn apart
And has totally shredded what was once your heart
There is a place that you can go
I've been there, I know it's so
When you're so mixed up you don't know what to do
Just go to Him, He's been waiting for you
He'll hide you and protect you and give you time to heal
There's nothing on this earth, my
friend, that will be more real
God's love is inexhaustible as He loves us as we are
With all our little hang-ups, He still out loves us by far
Only He is able to heal a heart
Only He can see that part
Just put your trust in the One who created you
He has already felt all that you are going through

God's Precious Light

Life is like a brilliant rainbow each and every day
Saturated with God's promises all along the way
No matter what the color of your day might turn out to be
It is His love and faithfulness that God wants you to see
Whether red days, yellow days, even green or blue
Just ask and He will always lead you all the way through
When you start allowing God's love into your heart
This will clean the dark things out and
give you a shiny new start
Then you will look at life with a brand-new sight
Because you will be reflecting God's precious light

How Effective Do You Want to Be?

Do you want everything that God's got
Or are you okay sitting like an old pine knot?
Do you want to see miracles left and right
Or do you think you do just fine in your own sight?
Don't you want to be sure when God talks to you
Or if it's Satan's voice who's actually slipped through?
Don't you want to send souls toward heaven's gate
Or do you watch them slip by into their hellish fate?
My friend God meant for you to be a soldier in this war
Not to sit and sulk and keep reliving some old scar
You have a special position to command
So set your feet firmly and take a stand
The Holy Spirit will go in front of you to guide
Jesus is always and ever at your side
God our Father will be behind you all the way
So what is it that keeps you from the victory today?

Do You Still Have a Conscience?

Do you feel guilty when you do something wrong
Or do you feel nothing while doing it all along?
This is a very serious situation my friend
It will tell you just how your life will end
Your conscience is a warning device God put inside of you
To let you know what's good and bad
and to make a choice that's true
If you do things that are wrong and don't feel a thing
Then let me tell you something
that'll make your ears sting
This means that your conscience has been seared
And it is toward hell your soul is being steered
The answer is not hard but is quite simple you know
Ask Jesus to save you and His great mercy He'll show

Your Words

Your words are very important so
be careful what you speak
Anything to do with life you must always seek
You always want to speak life and not death to someone
Even if you say you didn't mean it,
you were just having fun
Words will either justify or condemn you
You must always speak only what is true
God hears every word that you say
So don't think you can hide it away

God Loves You

You are so very precious in God's sight
No matter what you've done or what your fight
He wants you to know He loves you just as you are
You don't have to keep standing off so very far
Jesus gave His life especially for you
Knowing every single thing that you would ever do
He still loved you knowing that you might sin
So you could still have that choice to God to come in
So please don't turn and say, "I've just done too much"
Because my dear friend, there is no such
He only hates the sin and not you
So please come let Him make you new
Don't wait thinking it is too late
He wants to change your fate
If you could only see just how much He loves you and me
You would run to Him on bended knee
Please don't let your time run out
I promise, He will accept you, without one single doubt!

Do You Want Revival?

Are you willing to pay the price
Or do you want something that's just nice?
Are you tired of this world's sin
As each day it starts all over again?
Do you do anything to start a change
Or do you turn your head and think it strange?
Do you think I'm just one person what can I do?
All changes start with a single action that can be you
Are you willing to pray and fast
Standing unto the last?
If you don't want to pay the price my friend
Then you have no right to complain in the end
The flesh is weak and sometimes we fear
God is your strength and is always here
Make a choice today what you will do
God will enable you and see you through

Don't Withhold from God

Have you given your life to God above
And truly done it with your love
Maybe you've held back a tiny bit
Thinking God would not mind it
Ananias and Sapphira thought they would too
In their hearts they were untrue
Because of this they dropped dead
They withheld from God and were mislead
Don't keep part of your life but give it all
You don't want Him to answer in part when you call

Michael and Jackie

My heart perpetually loves the both of you
There's nothing on earth that I would not do
We three are a part of Mom and Dad
Yet another extension of God's work to add
I know you both will make them proud
As you learn to follow God and not the crowd
You both must make choices each day
No matter what your friends might say
Does God approve the choices that you make
Or do you ever stop to think about
the chance you might take
Each choice has either good or bad rewards behind it
Good or bad which return does your choice get
I pray this day God put an excessive hunger in your heart
To God you will give your all and not just a part
You will be miserable until you seek His face
But you will have great joy and peace
as you come to this place
Remember life is like a vapor it doesn't last long

The things you do and see are temporary
and are only a lifelong
Do the things you say and do help people to see the Lord
Or do they never see until it's too late
and they have Satan's reward?
My brothers you each have a special
work that must be done
It was handed down to us through our
parents and from God's Son
From our neglect let there not be one soul lost
There are many to be won whatever the cost

Do You Care About Your Friends

I know you were raised that drinking wasn't wrong
It was all right to dance and to hear a good ole song
But what's going to happen one day
When the Lord Himself will say
Yes child you've made it in
You've never let go of me from within
But just look at all of these souls on my left hand
They would be saved if you'd only made a stand
Into outer darkness they now will be cast
Some were your friends in the times past
Yes they are scared and very angry too
You see the one I chose to lead them to me was you
There are many souls you have let slip by
Just to ease your fear of what others
would think, if you should try
You see if you are saved Jesus is alive
in you and you should be dead
And if you're dead in Christ a dead
man's fears cannot be fed

If you are saved and yet in your life this isn't so
Then my friend, please, take a look just so you will know
You might not be where you thought you were at
The devil will so gradually draw you
away and leave you blind as a bat
Always take inventory of your actions
and what's in your heart
And compare them to God's Word so you'll never depart
Then ask Him to work through you to win the lost
So your friends can be saved instead
of paying a hellish cost

What Is Wrong?

My soul within me is in deep distress
In agony it screams with extreme unrest
I can see many ugly things being released from within
All of the hurts from a world of sin
What is all this that I see?
Oh please, my Lord, please forgive me
Could it be I've tried to live for you on my own
So you've removed the scales so that I could be shown?
Yes Lord I remember praying for a pure heart
This is it, this is how it must all start
For You to bring them up and then out
You feel and see them as they follow this route
I've seen and felt this I know that it's true
I must stand firm as you carry me all the way through
I do not want to be a hypocrite though
I want all and not just a part let it be so

Let Me See You as You Are

Lord I want to see who you really are
Not to keep looking at you through some old scar
I must see you as you would have me to
I know if I don't I can't go on through
For a while I've known something wasn't quite right
But I did not know that it was my own sight
The load has been heavy because I have seen you wrong
It makes the way so weary and dreadfully long
No wonder discouragement is always close by
Knowing gradually, I'll grow weary and too tired to try
I thought I had to do everything just right
Or else you'd be mad at me and keep me from your light
I was always beating my own self up inside
Thinking, "You'd better get it right or
His face from you He'll hide"
My only desire my Father is to please you
To be filled and poured out with all that is true
I don't want to hinder or limit you in any way
Allow your fullness to flow through me just as you say

Show Me

Father, please help me, show me the right way
My soul has been cast down and crushed as a piece of clay
I know that I am human and ever so weak
If you'll just fill me up I'll promise always to seek
There is no power of myself to help or heal
Even with me knowing that this is your will
No matter what it takes Lord let your will be done
There are too many lost souls that must be won

To My Mate

You are the one sent to me from long ago
A loving gift from God to me below
Molding and shaping us one for the other
To fulfill all through this dad and this mother
I can look all around and never see
That no one else could ever be
Only you with your special heart
Does perfectly fit every part
God knew only you could help me see
Unconditional love from a man to me
Since I've never seen this from a man
It made it hard to understand
If I slip you're not ugly nor do you holler
You don't try to control me with an invisible collar
I know I don't fully understand God's love just yet
But "oh" the love He sends through you, that I get
I thank God for you and all that He has done
And thank you for keeping God in
your life as number one

Tragedy and Relief

Oh tragedy of tragedies my soul does cry out
This loss of my precious parents is what this is about
A part of me seems to be lost and wondering around
Desperately and longingly waiting to
hear just one slight sound
Then there is a part which is everlastingly
thankful to my God above
That He keeps them safe and has enveloped
them with His inexhaustible love

(Thank you, my Heavenly Father, for the
ability to love and appreciate my
parents whom you've shared with me for a
time. They are no longer in my past
but they are in my future—eternally.)

No Time to Waste

Please lead me God so that my time will have no waste
It is you and heaven that I want for all to taste
Ever keep me walking straight
I want none to show up late
Precious Lord fulfill in me all that you did call
Only by Your mighty hand will I stand and shall not fall
There are so many people in bondage
and in chains so very thick
Silent, but deadly, as in different
areas they become more sick
Ready this vessel Lord to be fully used by you
Let not one speck remain that could ever be untrue
I know time is short and I cannot hesitate
It's the enemies' hold, in people's lives, I want to eliminate
Give me the vision Lord of what you'd have me to do
And I know you'll give me the ability
as you see me through

Are There Idols in Your Life?

Is there anything in your life that might take away
Even a part of your service from God today?
Is there a person you might hold up too high
That you have no time with God to comply?
Are you in awe as your favorite singer is singing
That your devotion is to them and not to God clinging?
Are you held captive by your own television
That work goes undone and causes strife and division?
Do you get so caught up in helping everyone out
That your own family has had to go without?
Does sports consume you body and soul
And have you in its complete control?
Does money seem to drive you and
is the object of your goal?
This puts God second and it will be
the destruction of your soul
Maybe you're one who is caught up in constant spending
Little or a lot with your cause always defending
Idolatry in any form God hates it so

It keeps you from heaven and will destroy your very soul
When you give anyone or anything a greater devotion
You've cut yourself off from God and
there'll be no promotion
God must be first in all that you do my friend
Then you'll enjoy all the other things in balance and blend

To You Who Will Stand

Standing tall and standing fast
As did the Godly men of our past
We've lost a lot through the years
From lack of knowledge and many fears
We must regain the ground that we have lost
Active in prayer and fasting whatever the cost
My heart beats proud for all of you
Who stands for truth and won't fall through
We are God's mouth, hands and feet
There should not be any defeat
The world God already overcame
We should all be doing the very same

Judge Roy Moore
Montgomery, Alabama
Gov. Fob James
This poem came when Judge Roy Moore was standing
against a Federal Judges order to remove the Ten
Commandments from the lobby of the Alabama

Judicial Building. Governor Fob James stood with and behind Judge Moore. I have never met these two special men but I love their stand for what is right and it shows just a portion of their heart for the things of God and a compassion for true justice for the people. Our justice system came from the Bible and it is slowly being degraded by Political Correctness.

And to all who will take a stand on what is right. If all the Christian people will come into unity and make a stand and pray; quit letting the enemy cause us to fight each other and steal everything from under us, we, by prayer and action through God can turn things around so God can heal our nation and continue to bless other nations with the gospel, food, clothing, and medical supplies.

Empty Me Lord

I have no time to be full of myself
Nor to waste time like a book on a shelf
All that I am I give unto you
Step by step as you lead me through
Let all that is useless in me be emptied out
Don't leave one thing that would cause a soul to doubt
Remove me Lord from myself, don't let me stay
I am usually the one always in my way
The more of me that is cast to the side
The more you can fill me so I may fully abide
Only through you, precious Spirit, will I be able to do
The work set before me and to be faithful and true

Teach Me to Teach
My Children Lord

It is only You Lord who is able to teach
The parents for their child's soul to reach
I trust not in myself but only in you
As you teach me to teach them to be completely true
Only You Lord know exactly what it will take
For each child a successful life to make
Just as you deal differently with each of us
Let me learn to listen carefully and not just to fuss
Thank You for sharing the boys with me for a while
As you teach me to teach them to go over each mile
Fulfill your plan for them don't let them fall away
But hold tightly to them till you call them home to stay

You Are My Everything

You are my strength you are my light
You are my breath both day and night
Only through you am I able to truly live
A life that is pleasing and willing to give
Only through you am I able to change
The things I once knew and now are so strange
Truly you are leading me up the steps of glory
Not always easy but yet it is a priceless story

Time with You

Lord I need more time to spend with you
To allow you to do what you will do
A special word, a special touch
Nothing will ever compare to such
You meet with me Lord every time
And sometimes give me a word in special rhyme
You are so precious and priceless too
Oh give me time, more time with you
The more time I spend the more I seem to need
As the thirsting hunger of a young fertile seed
No matter what happens in this life of mine
Let Your Spirit so draw me, oh let Him shine
As you whisper, "Come spend some time with me"
Let me always hear, for that is where I want to be

A Love That Will Never End!

Are you one that has been hurt and has grown cold
Because of a broken heart from a love of old
My love will not ever be broken from you
No matter what you've done or what you will do
If you mess up, don't pull away from me
A true love will love you through anything you see
I am always here for you and love you so
I'll not ever leave you no matter where you go
I know for you who are hurt it's hard to believe
You say, "It's too good to be true, you too will deceive"
But I say unto you this very day
It is I who created you all the way
My love is greater than any you've known
If you'll let me, the price has clearly been shown
But you must ask me to come into your life
I won't push my way in, I'm not one of strife
Just ask me and I'll come in unto you
And restore and heal all you've been through

You Lord Are the Utmost within My Soul

You Lord are the utmost within my soul
Onward leading me always toward the goal
There's not one other who could do what you have done
To give us forgiveness and life eternal
through your faithful Son
Daily you grow more and more precious to me
As you lovingly remove hindrances from before me to see
Yes you are the utmost within my soul
Onward leading me always toward the goal
I dare not take credit from any one thing
I know from you all life and good does continually spring
You are my very life from deep within
You are my every breath as I breathe in
You are the utmost within my soul
Onward leading me always toward the goal

Teach and Change Me Lord

Forgive me Lord for the words I speak
Don't even begin to touch the peak
Oh so glorious are You Lord and I praise you so
Though hindered by mere words my heart does truly show
Continually growing and always reaching
Striving toward and never ceasing
The closer I get the greater my hunger does grow
And the more of you sweet Lord
into me you do always sow
Please give me the ability to know
how to better honor you
Because I know without you there
is not one thing I could do
Oh, that I may see all things the way you do
And speak only that which is but true
I wait patiently Lord for you to change
All that is in me that to you is strange
Please leave not even a vapor from within

That could ever cause me to hurt you by sin
However hard the trials and the tribulation
As long as you bring me to that final destination

Thank You Father for Sharing Mom and Dad with Us

So precious were the arms you made
to hold me oh so tight
Also the kind hands that taught me what
was wrong and what was right
Her loving words are ever entwined within my very being
As they multiply and are given out to all those I am seeing
So precious was he that taught me work until it's done
To do a work completely as if unto God's Son
He put a desire in me deep within my soul
To know God and His fullness this is my very goal
So thankful am I of You Lord and what you've given me
Your character shined brightly through Mom
and Dad and helped me clearly see
All the love and care that they did instill
Was just a tiny portion of what you really feel
Thank You Father for sharing them with us for a time
They taught us about you and those
golden stairs that we will climb

Thank You for that blessed hope which
knows not time no more
Till we see our precious loved ones
as we meet on heaven's shore

To Know You More

Oh how the hunger does burn within me
Steadily reaching upward into thee
To know you more, moment by day
To cling to You in all that You say
The screaming pains of my spirit, only you can quiet
The flood of tears that come, only you can dry it
Oh and yes, only your precious touch
Can comfort and console me so very much
I know I don't know your full love toward me
But oh, so awesome, is what I do see
All of my needs I use to pray for
But if I have the full of you, I need no more
You cause all else to fall into place
And that there's a certain reason for all that we face

Your Vessels

Let this vessel never try to use the power that created it
But know without the power it cannot move one little bit
I know you've created many vessels
for different types of works
Help me Lord to never put down a
vessel for odd little quirks
Help me to pray for each vessel that they be tried and true
So they won't break under pressure while
doing what you've called them to do
Please don't let the vessels jump out to start a work to soon
Before being tried and seasoned so they
won't blow up like a balloon
Let your vessels be patient so you
can do the work in each one
So they won't leak or break but only
pour out the fullness of Your Son

You Are the Key

Oh Lord it seems that I've sought for so long
All of the keys to be closer to you as well as to be strong
Over and over I would start again
Only to find myself back where I did begin
Ever so zealous and wanting to please
It seemed even the knockdowns came with ease
As the years ran on something seemed wrong
I thought I was doing it right but I'd lost my song
What could it be Lord I just don't understand?
This can't be the life for me that you had planned
The key, my child, is in your heart when I came in
That key you've used blindly ever now and then
Only this key can unlock all other doors you see
This key works only when you spend time daily with me
I am the key that takes you from glory to glory
The key to each gate that takes you up a story
If you want to come up higher seek my face
I long to unlock the blessings for you at each new place
Oh come and see I have so much for you
All I ask is to put me first in all that you do

Fully Consume Me Lord

Help me Lord to die a complete death
So I may be fully consumed by your life-giving breath
Living and breathing in a new atmosphere
I can hardly wait, it's almost here
To be fully consumed, to be a flame of fire
This is my continual and burning desire
Oh how I want to be obedient to everything you speak
Always and forever only you does my heart seek
May flames from this fire always reach out and touch
The thirsting and hungering souls you love so very much
May it so burn up all that's in the way
So they can see You Lord in a greater way

The Greater You Love, the Greater the Pain

The deeper your love for people that's real
The deeper the pain from them you'll feel
The shallow heart always says, "What about me?"
While the heart with depth looks past its pain to see
Only the love of God in a heart is able to keep
Hardness from coming in and settling down deep
His love keeps you from being critical and trying to judge
And even helps you from holding onto a grudge
A heart is very capable of great love or great wrong
The choice is in each heart no matter if
you're weak or if you're strong
Do you think about how you will affect others
with what you do and what you say
Or do you set out to do whatever you
want in whatever kind of way?

Rescue Me Lord

Father they are again gathering together against me
Oh please help me I know that you can see
This has gone on for so very long
But it is you who helps me to be strong
I wish them no harm I just want them to quit
Only You Lord can persuade them to stop it
With their many lies they lay their traps
Hoping that they will destroy me as it snaps
It sometimes seems way too much to bear
But still in yet I know you care
I forgave them Lord as you did ask
This in itself was a very hard task
No matter how much harm they seem to do
I do know that you will carry me through
You already saved me from hell once before
And I know this plea you'll not ignore
You did not save me to leave me here
So, in Jesus name, I rebuke the fear
I know you will do what you have planned
For who is able to stop your mighty hand

I know you will bring about what you have said
So, in Jesus name, I rebuke the dread
In Your time Lord You will confound all those against me
And all looking on will clearly see
It is you who has rescued me once again
And who has balanced out the scales of sin

My Life Is Not Mine to Take

My heart seems to have been taken away
Where now only pain and agony does replay
I seem to be in some deep black hole
And the only sound is the torturing of my soul
Death sounds so sweet at this point in time
And continually sings to me with his rhyme
Only You Lord can dry my tears
Only you can make the darkness disappear
But I know my life is not mine to take
Heaven is the destination I want to make
For You Lord are the only one to know
How to get out of this place and which way to go
You have never failed me any time before
Always strengthening as you did restore
Please help me keep my mind stayed on you
In doing this I will have a new view
Let Your Psalms wash over my wounded heart
Healing me thoroughly in every part
Oh that I may understand your love toward me
No walls between us but only you that I see

Thankfulness

My precious Lord my heart is bursting with thankfulness
For all you have shown and taught for my happiness
Even through many a sad and painful trial
You've always walked me through each and every mile
I shall always and ever praise Your Holy Name
As I grow in you my heart does most proudly exclaim
I will never be able to thank you enough
For the good things as well as for the tough
No matter how good or how hard I will not stop
Until your work in me is done and you take me to the top

Just a Vessel

I'm just a vessel Lord being filled with your anointed rain
To be poured out on the hearts and souls
of bodies wrecked with pain
Let all my flesh be cast aside
With only you in me to abide
I do this very day proclaim
Only in Jesus's mighty name
The bound and the oppressed be set free
From this day forth through eternity
Let it be told from coast to coast
Jesus is the Lord of hosts
I call forth a greater revelation
For God's children in every nation

I Want You to Be My Heart

I want You Lord to be my very heart
To pump your life throughout me to each and every part
Let everything that you are transfuse into me
That you saturate and permeate even all that I see
Let your ways become my very nature in all that I do
That your work is done completely and
to the full when it is through
Let me so burn with your fire that I'm totally ablaze
Always and forever giving you the glory and the praise
Save all of those drawn in by Your Holy fire
And give to each one a deep, eternal, burning desire

So Much Keeps Happening

Lord so much keeps happening when will it ease?
It is only you that I want to please
Things happen and hurt me no matter where I turn
Please explain Lord, teach me, I'm so willing to learn
Child, how many times have you asked me in the past
To be able to trust me totally and
completely even unto the last
I didn't even have to think, this was a
deep desire within my being
Many, many times Lord I answered,
please, help me continue seeing
My child how can you learn to trust
me in all areas of your life
Unless they are shaken to see if you
have peace or if you have strife
Through each area you learned to walk in peace
Now you know this is the only place you can live in ease
And since you learned these lessons the hard way
You now guard the peace you fought for many a day
So anything in your life that is being shaken

Stand firm and hold tight to me and
only the bad will be taken
Look back child on your life and you'll find
You're much stronger now in spirit and mind

Hebrews 12:26–28 (Amplified)

Where Did You Go, Lord?

Oh Lord, what happened, where did you go?
I don't like what I see, please help me to know
I do not desire to pray or seek
This is not right, it seems so bleak
I do not even care to read your word
Now isn't that just quite absurd?
I don't desire to help anybody out
Or to even think what your word's about
The only desire is to do whatever I want to do
And I surely don't want to be bothered
with what others are going through
Okay Lord, what is going on here, please explain?
Only you are able to show me and please make it plain
My child, I drew back my presence from
you so you could clearly see
That there is nothing in you that
would want to ever live for me
It is "my presence only" that gives you those desires
And it is by my breath that fans the
sparks into the flaming fires

I Must Have More!

Lord, my insides ache for more of you
A greater revelation I must have to carry me through
I want nothing less than to walk in
what you've bought for me
No longer in part but in all fullness do I want to see
For how can I teach others to stand on Your Holy Word
If my understanding is sometimes a little bit blurred
I know Lord this is not at all your fault
Nor anything you have or have not taught
But solely mine for not seeking you enough
May I be soaked with hunger for
you no matter how tough
It is divine health I choose to walk in
And not to give my body over to sickness or sin
I choose to walk in the fullness of your authority
Instead of being walked on like the majority
I choose only your fullness working in and through me
And nothing in the natural will ever move where we'll be

Give me this day Father, a greater
revelation of who you are
And use me in whatever way you will, near or far

No Death Dwelleth Here

Oh my great and powerful God
It is with you I'm clothed and shod
Absolutely no death dwelleth here
Only your peace is allowed to steer
You are all in all "Life" itself
And that very life is inside myself
So no death doth dwell in here
Only the seal of Your Spirit ever so near
Since your life is on the inside of me
Death simply cannot dwell here, it just can't be
Death and life can never dwell together
So let God have your death and He'll
give you His life forever

Only in Him

Oh how my love does exceedingly grow
As Your love through me does continually flow
Always expanding and so heavenly divine
Love is, as always, most surely the sign
How do you know if your walk is right
You simply follow His life giving light
Only in Him is He able to give
Life more abundantly that He wants us to live

God's Fullness—
Not Parts and Pieces

To walk with you to hear your voice
This is up to me to make this choice
But there are so many who think this can't be so
They think this passed away a long, long time ago
They will never have what they don't believe
It is only then that they can receive
I choose to have all of you
Not just parts that I've picked through
In God's fullness is so much for us to learn
Just like the road of life going round a new turn
A little scary because it's new
But as you walk in it, it becomes true blue
Each new level with God starts the same
As you walk with Him, new ground you'll gain
So do not fear what is out there and unknown
He instructs us and guides us in all He has shown

Do not think because something is
awkward it's not for us today
All it takes is a seeking heart for His
fullness and He'll show you the way

Hidden Rejection

Oh why my soul are you cast down again?
You have not purposely partaken in any sin
You're up for a while and then you're down
And always on the inside do you wear a frown
You always seem to smile on the outside
And no longer from the pain are you able to hide
Lord, help me to know what this could be
Only you know and can help me to see
Rejection, you say, buried deep within
From an early age it did begin
Always trying to do everything just right
To gain approval in the people's sight
Work, work, work but don't make one mistake
Such a heavy load without a single break
Try, try, try and give it your absolute best
If you make a mistake, there will be no rest
No matter what I did it seemed so bleak
I've not ever found what I did seek
When people hurt me, I just shut that door

And think, "I'll not do anything with them anymore"
Anyway, it seems, I never fit in with anybody much
And the one I did was taken from my clutch
Please help me Lord, I don't want to live a miserable life
I want so much to be happy and above the strife
I know this is the beginning of what I see
As you brought it out and have shown it to me
Deliver me Lord from the roots of rejection
And reveal to me your undying love and sincere affection
I do not want my happiness to depend
on what people say or do
But I want to be permanently fixed, in and through you

Do You Believe?

God is a mighty God and always will be
It is only by His presence that you clearly see
He does outstanding works that no one can explain
And boggles the mind of those who rejects His life as gain
Why is this such a problem to believe or not too?
There's no loss, but only gain, as you walk in what is true
Have you thought," what is it that's
in me that does not believe,
Could it be I was not taught, so I cannot receive?
It is the enemy of your soul that twists it all into junk
And then whispers to you, it's just a bunch of bunk
So in frustration you throw up your hands
And the enemy leads you down an easier
road, according to his own plans
The enemy promises you ecstasy as he lies to your soul
And will never tell you of his horrible, vindictive goal
He wants you wiped off of the face of the earth
And if he could have, he would have done it at birth
You mean nothing to him in any sort of way

You're just a pawn, he wants to use, to make his own play
You see since God created all of mankind
This was the only thing the devil could find
To hurt God the most was what he was after
So now on mankind he wreaks havoc and disaster
Then he causes some to believe God did the bad
And causes God's heart to be so sad
Doubt and unbelief is what he plants in people's hearts
To build a wall to keep God and you apart
Do not let him keep you away from true life
He wants you to burn with him and all of his strife
Just call out to Jesus you don't have to wait
He created you and heaven is a much better fate

What Is Hindering Me from Happiness?

Where is the happiness I so long to see
Where is the abundance you promised me
I am saved Lord without a doubt
Doing all I know to do to bring it about
I stand and stand and stand on Your Holy Word
Until sheer frustration makes me want to fly off like a bird
I know it is not You Lord for You cannot lie
But at times I think I can't do anything
right and I just would like to die
I try and try and try till I became literally exhausted
It seems even my feelings are shut
off and need to be defrosted
Sometimes I'm lost for days at a time I find
While being thoroughly tortured in my body and mind
This is not what you gave your life for
I know it's supposed to be abundantly more
What is it, Lord, what do you see

Please help me with it as you show it to me
You bring up the woman you gave to be my mother
So utterly precious there could be no other
Yes she did have an abundance of pain in her life
Which cut away the happiness like some sharp knife
I remember from the time I was very small
I always wanted to take on me the pain of it all
Wanting so desperately to take her past
So maybe just a little joy would be able to last
To me she deserved all of the very best
My heart wanted to give her the
world as her treasure chest
Please forgive me Father, I hear what you say
Now I know I handled it in the wrong way
Only you are able to fix this kind of a pain
And turn it around so it becomes our gain
You already took upon yourself all pain ever to be felt
And all battles of the flesh as in Gethsemane You knelt
I repent Lord for what I tried to do
I tried to do your part instead of giving it to you
I receive your forgiveness and a complete healing
So that the enemy cannot continue on stealing
I unknowingly and willingly took on a generational curse
To continue bearing all the pain that was in her purse

Physically and mentally the pain was passed down to me
How thankful I am Lord that you've helped me to see
Please show me Lord if there's anything else
That would hinder me from you inside myself

Please Help Me Lord

Please help me Lord, it's happening again
This horrible tormenting battle will I ever win
To the depths of despair my soul does sink
It is a battle just for my mind to think
There's so much I don't understand at all
And every time I turn around it seems I fall
I cannot get anything at all to work right
Everything is constantly a struggle and a fight
I have been separated from most everyone
This is of itself no part of fun
From the one that did remain
Did I receive a vast amount of pain
Accusing me of something I did not do
While saying God told them so and it was true
From that moment it felt my heart was cut out
And I could not feel anything from without
My first thought was to strike back
But that would be more pain I would have to pack
I do not want to hurt the friend that I love so

No matter how much pain, on me, she did bestow
I forgive her Lord for what she did give
Forgive me also and help me to live
A life without cleansing often becomes stale
And will eventually become a tough, hard shell
So if you have hurts, don't keep them trapped inside
Find a way to release them so they can't run and hide
If you don't, the roots will grow way down deep
And at any time the hurt and bitterness can take a leap
For me the answer seems to flow without a doubt
As soon as I get my pen and paper out
The Lord does always help me go through
So I write it down so it will help you

A Deceiving Thought

I did not know nor did I realize
The simple reason why my heart cries
Confusion is what usually would come about
No matter how much I prayed day in and day out
Deliver me Lord, did I finally pray
From this thing that's in my way
Remove everything that would hinder me from you
And help me to receive all that is true
You say it's a thought that's hindered me so
That has been with me from a long time ago
A thought that's crippled me and made me blue
And kept me from having the full of you
The longer this thought does get to stay
The stronger he becomes and gets his way
As he goes unnoticed his strength does grow
Always trying to weaken my faith while he lies low
While circulating himself through
my mind again and again
He keeps your thinking poisoned so you can't ever win

This "thought" becomes a mind-set in your thinking
And has to be changed or you'll continue on sinking
The thought that I've carried since I was very small
All the money and good things were
for others and not for me at all
I was taught to always give and not to take
This I found is a big mistake
How can I give if I've not learned to receive?
Now I see I can truly believe
I didn't think I deserved good things
From the thought inside always pulling those strings
I deserve them only because of what you did on Calvary
All because of the love and blessings
you wanted to give me
So now you've shown me I gladly say
I fully receive everything you have for me today
So pour it out, every little bit
You've already paid in full for all of it
Please forgive me Lord for saying I cannot receive
All because of a tiny thought who did, so greatly, deceive
I Thank You Father, I shall no longer
be hindered in this place
But I shall continue on in your loving mercy and grace

Help Us to Understand

Only You Lord can set us free
From the binding chains we do not see
I've learned that truth in itself is of no good
Unless that truth is clearly understood
How can you have that which you do not understand?
That's why many are without in what
should be their promised land
Thirteen years it's taken for me to be able to see
The place God really wants and desires me to be
When all was lost by the sin of Adam and Eve
Jesus became the sacrifice for us so we again could receive
Since Jesus came and purchased everything back
Why is it that so many still live in so much lack?
We have the blood bought right to
live the way God meant
To live and enjoy God and creation to the full extent
So remember to pray for understanding as you read
And God will enlighten you to fill your every need

Press On

Though there are many with hurts so very deep
We are still counted as His little sheep
Though many of those hurts go from light to some so bold
Many are hidden out of sight and simply go untold
Press on my precious friend don't get stuck in the pain
Or you'll sink as the hurt will continue to rule and to reign
Every day, everything, is a choice you know
So choose wisely for the direction that you want to go
Do you choose to replay the sorrow
over and over in your mind;
That will literally keep you a prisoner
and your head in a bind
Or do you choose to let go of all of your past
So you can receive God's fullness that will far outlast
Press on my friend from this unhappy place
And let God pour upon you His mercy and His grace

Raise Your People Up

Raise your people up Lord and set them free
Cut loose the yokes and cords of iniquity
People are saved but live with invisible chains
They smile but are full of deep, torrential pains
Many are able to handle it for quite a long while
Until the load of problems become way too great a pile
At this point weariness and confusion take hold
And doubt slips in to try to remold
Then everything becomes such a big mess
And brings about a great deal of stress
At this point there are some who walk away
From a lack of understanding of what Your Word does say
Raise your people up Lord and set them free
Cut loose the yokes and cords of iniquity
Reveal to Your people Lord, oh let them see
Exactly what you wrote and meant it to be
Only by You Lord are we able to know
The truth, height and depth of love you want to show
Remove everything from us that would ever hinder
And help us to always, completely, surrender

Pain in the Sea of Life

Swirling and sloshing shoving and bashing
Ever so steady does life go on dashing
Pain now daily does continually flow
And seems to be drowning my very soul
Sometimes the pain is so strong, I cannot think
As life goes on I seem to sink
I need your help Lord or else I'll drown
I know on my own I will go down
I know there are others in worse shape than me
And I thank you dearly for helping me to see
There are many others in much greater pain
And you can turn it around and cause it to be gain
Nothing is ever easy in this sea of life
Beauty can't be felt if you haven't felt the strife
Like the water washing trash off of its shore
And leaving in its place pretty shells and so much more
So cleaning our insides up doesn't feel so very nice
But oh, the pretty things left, after we pay the price

You Justify Me

Thank You Lord that you justify me
You don't see me the way that I use to be
By the Blood of Jesus in Your sight
You have caused me to walk a right
I don't have to work to be okay
But only believe in what you did say
No matter how big of a mess I had in my life
All the problems the battles and all of the strife
Only you, precious Lord, only You
Can show me how I need to walk through
Thank You Lord for setting me free
And causing me to walk in all that you bought for me

Let's Get Back to the Spirit and Power

People have gotten so caught up in all the "mechanics"
If you don't do it just this way, then everyone panics
We have tried so hard to reason and work things out
To get people saved and healed to where there is no doubt
But still there is something not quite right
Something is still missing in this fight
God is pouring out a great revelation
Only to those who are tuned in to His station
But don't expect it to just drop down on you
To seek and crave Him first and
foremost is what you should do
Then you are tuned into the right frequency to receive
All that God has stored up for you then simply believe
Do not skip a day of tuning in to Him
Because the frequency will start to
fade and will become dim
Once you've found this secret place and its Holy treasure

You will grow in every area of your
life, far beyond measure

Then when you are faithful with this one precious jewel

God will then release through you, His mighty Power Tool

Once this happens the most important
thing to you will be

To keep and protect the Holy Spirit
that God has given thee

Don't Seek Your Own Need

Oh my precious Lord please forgive me
You are so awesome as you show me how to be
While always praying and asking for my healing
I did not see how the enemy did keep on stealing
How thankful I am as you open up my eyes
And teach me yet another step to be more wise
If I'll just keep my eyes focused on you
And do all that You put before me to do
If I'll just pray for those who have a need
I'll reap a harvest from this very seed
When my eyes are kept off of me
No matter what my need might be
Then Lord my body has to fall in line
No matter the trap the enemy did design
My body then does not have a choice
It will be healed as I do rejoice

America and God

So many battles and wars have been fought
By their blood this nation has been bought
So precious is the freedom that we all share
To be able to do whatever your heart's care
So sad is it now that so many have forgotten
The Godly heritage from whence we were begotten
Things are too easy for them today
And they have grown blind and gone astray

Now let me tell you a similar story
One that is greater yet and full of glory
Jesus too through battles and wars did fight
And had to go through His darkest night
By His blood your soul has been bought
Please don't let His life's blood be for naught
He bought back for you the freedom of choice
So you can have life and freely rejoice

Here again is it sad that so many have forgotten

The Godly heritage from whence we were begotten
Why must you wait till life is almost cut off
Before you call out to the One that before you did scoff
God wants you to be blessed beyond measure
He has great riches to give you from His treasure
You are running from the One who has
the power to help you break
Every chain of bondage from your soul to take

Deliver Your People Lord

Never let me cease to seek for you
Forever keep my heart tried and true
Only You Lord are able to keep
Each one of your little sheep
Deliver then your people from the enemy's snare
That has robbed them and taken away their share
Some have grown so weary and so weak
And have even forgotten how to seek
Some have been caught up for so long
They are deceived and think nothing is wrong
The enemy lets them have just a taste ever so often
To reduce to a medium their will, as
it does continually soften
It is time Lord for Your People to be set free
You're the only living and awesome
God that can cause them to see
Let it not be in vain what Jesus did upon the cross
He did not give His life so we could have loss
Cause us to see what we must do

Remove all hindrances between us and you
There is such great wealth in the kingdom that we are in
Yet most never partake because of the snares of sin
Send us your wisdom and knowledge to help us know
At each new day, which direction to go
Help us to walk in your love each day
So you can touch others along the way

Possess Me Lord

Possess me fully Lord, my entire being
I'd rather be blind if I cannot continue through you seeing
Only because of what you chose to do for me
Can I reap life forever more abundantly
It is so true, I am no longer my own
I am a seed, that into you, has been sown
No longer do I ask myself, "What do I do?"
I am yours now and I wait upon you
It is no longer up to me which way I go
My life is in your hands and you will show
I pour myself out Lord for you to use
And only by your strength am I able to choose
I want no strength of my own, it is false and unsure
Only your strength is true and will help me to endure
Forever keep me hungering and thirsting for you
Always possessing through me all that you will do

Thank You for the Fires

Thank You for the fires that I have to go through
Or I would never be able to get closer to you
They do get awful hot and drain my strength from me
This is exactly what you wanted me to see
My strength is taken and you replace it with yours
To make me a stronger vessel and able to endure
Thank You Father for Your heavenly fires
Burn out everything in me that would hinder your desires
Search me with your fire Lord, set ablaze my very soul
Use me in any way Lord I give you full control

Death and Resurrection

As you show me each thing that does hinder me so
I must not struggle with it but let it go
I must die to it at the cross and leave it there
Where you did die to all of the pain that you did bear
This was a very hard thing for you to do
But you knew you had to see it completely through
You knew on the other side of death,
there was endless power
But still it was heart rending for you in your final hour
Oh, but praise You Jesus, You did show the way
Power only comes as I die to things each day
As I die to a problem I am then raised up with you
"Resurrection can only come if the death is true"
Little by little am (I) totally emptied of all
That would ever hinder me any when the Master does call
Only you know Lord what it is I need to die to
So that you can draw me up, even closer unto you

The Altar

The greatest altar that there ever has been
Was the cross at Calvary that paid for our sin
The Lamb of God was laid upon the alter called a cross
And did pay in full for us, while He suffered great loss
So if you are tired of problems in your life
They have you frantic, confused or in strife
You need not only seek for a church
An alter can be where you are right
now, you don't have to search
Everything in life is very much a choice
Do you choose to stay bitter or choose to rejoice
"You must hold fast to your confession
once you lay it down
Or it will follow close behind you
and come right back around"
Some things are not easy at all to put to death
That's why we must speak God's Word
from His life-giving breath
Remember, God's Word is alive, active and full of power

And you must speak it boldly in your final hour
Then you shall see the victory over each thing
And you will be free to shout and to sing

Note: The line, "You need not only seek for a church," does not mean we shouldn't go to church. God says in Hevrews 10:25 KJV that we should not forsake the assembling of ourselves together as believers. This line means that you don't have to wait to get to church to get God's help with a problem. You can stop anywhere you are and talk to Him and leave that problem with Him. Any place you pray becomes an alter.

Focus

Listen and think on this thing that I have to say
I want you to focus on something that you love today
Maybe it's a sports game or a TV show
Something you don't like to be interrupted
while doing, you know
Some of you get downright mad
When your focus is broken it can get bad
Now, think on the time you spend with me today
Some don't ever focus on me that way
Every little thing seems to draw your attention
Oh, and did I forget to mention
Remember during a football game,
someone stepped in front of you
Your blood pressure rose and you got
angry because they broke your view
Why do you not fight and get that
angry to keep your focus on me
For I am the only One who can give you life eternally
All these things that you are focused
on shall be no more one day

They shall all cease to be as soon as time does hear me say
Then on Judgment Day when you stand
before me and I ask you why
What will be your focus then? For it will be too late to try
So stop and rethink where your focus is right now
If you will ask me to help you I will show you how
Some get focused on pain that happened in their past
They become prisoners of war and some do not last
Whatever you focus on, it always grows more clear
Good or bad, focus will always draw you near
So keep your focus and I will continually draw you to me
Always unfolding myself and allowing you to see

Choose to Die to Self

The more of yourself that you try to protect
The more of God that you will neglect
You get offended by a word or a look
And refuse to even think it could have been mistook
There always seems to be someone not treating you right
You did nothing wrong, so you're ready to fight
Let's just stop and take a look at this situation
And see what God's Word says, upon examination
We must decrease ourselves more each day
So God can increase in us and have His way
Little by little we must learn to die
And give to Him that place of self that we call "I"
If we do not choose to lay it down
Then oppression and sorrow will abound
This will then humble us and help us to know
We must always "need Him" to help us grow
Once you've laid your life down you can't take it back
A dead man does not feel nor does he loose track

Psalm 107:39–43 (Amplified)

I have been crucified with Christ (in Him I have shared
His crucifixion); it is no longer "I" who
live, but Christ lives in me; and
the life I now live in the body I live by faith
in (and reliance on and complete
trust in) the Son of God, Who loved
me and gave Himself up for me.

Galatians 2:20 (Amplified)

Pain or Freedom?

Lord now do I truly see
The reason for all that is behind me
Each horrible thing that happened in my past
Helped to get me to this place at last
Even those things I thought I did hate
I did not understand why they were on my plate
Then you brought your word and you did show to me
What I had to do if I wanted to be free
It was up to me then, the choice was mine
Did I want to be free or stay hanging on a line?
How do I forgive those that are so mean and unfair?
My child, give them to me, so I can handle the care
This will set you free when you put them in my hand
For there is no evil thing that before me can stand
"I cannot do a thing until you release them to me
Because I have already given you the authority"
Lord I choose not to be bound by anything but you
Thank You for the grace and wisdom to see me through
Now I see the reason for all of that stuff

It kept me on my knees and off of my duff
Only You Lord can take the things that are so sad
And turn them into good when it did look so bad
Thank You Lord you are ever so sure
Steady your children and help them to endure

Reveal the Hidden Desires

Reveal to me Lord those hidden desires
That burst open with life from your flaming fires
Open them up Lord as you turn up the flame
"Do not cease, till I am never the same"
May my hunger and thirst grow each day
Do not ever let me have my way
Continually change me, do not ever stop
I do not want to miss even one little drop
Help me to walk in your balance, so I can walk straight
To lead all those who will, to heaven's home plate

Help Me Lord

Help me Lord to never think more
highly of myself than I ought
I've come through many heavy battles to
find the place that I have sought
The boldness you are giving me wants so much to lead
Others to this place that is of such great need
Yet I don't want to hurt or offend anyone along the way
So help me walk in wisdom and
balance each and every day
I never want to overstep any type of authority
So put down in my heart a tender sensitivity
I only want to please you with all I say and do
So remind me that it is me who must
humble myself before you

A Great Privilege

My Lord, my God, you are all knowing
Even polluted by evil does creation continue on showing
So ceaseless are you in your righteousness
That none can stand before you unless they confess
You have always held all might and power
Even unto this day and this very hour
So awesome is your power to create any and all
Yet, you give us a choice, when our name, you call
You give us this great privilege knowing
all that we have done wrong
Oh yes, you are a loving God that
does not make us go along
You did not make us to be robots, even though you could
This is such a depth of love that is hardly understood
Oh you are so ever increasingly awesome
Causing all who accept you to continually blossom
You called me to be your child even when I was in sin
Knowing the sin that I would do even after I came in
Oh, your mercy and grace does far exceed

My smallest or my greatest deed
You knew your love would change all of my ways
So we could fellowship all of my days
You are so exceedingly precious, I dare not lose
That anything against you I dare not choose

I'm Free

I'm free, I'm free, you have set me free
No longer does sin and sickness have its hold on me
I no longer have lack in any area of my life
Nor am I hindered by that old spirit of strife
I have fought against myself for so very long
Wracking my mind to see just what I was doing wrong
I knew all that you promised in Your Word You would do
But what was I doing wrong that it didn't come through
I thought maybe I should fast or pray even more
Then this might be the key to unlock the door
Maybe I'm doing something wrong I do not see
Oh please God, please, show it to me
Child, all these years you've tried to be so good
To receive all my promises, you have not understood
You came from a background where
you had to work and get it right
Or you would not be pleasing in anyone's sight
I am God who created all heaven and earth
It is I who called your name before it was given at birth

All My promises have been paid for in full
And working to receive them is against my rule
All that you must do my child, is to accept My Son
Then every promise that you read, know, that it is done
You do not need to cry, beg or plead
Simply receive by faith all that you need
It is all paid for, you don't have to do one thing
Accept to speak and expect it and then praise the King

Consumed

I am totally consumed by your desire
To be an ever-increasing and burning fire
Fire only burns when it has oxygen to breath
So it is in and to your presence that I must cleave
For in Your presence oxygen is so pure
Keeping me burning steadfast and sure
In Your presence life does always increase and grow
So it is you who increases that fire, I know
As long as I am consistently before you
My walk with you will be honest and true

I'm Going Through

I make a choice right here and now
I will not turn back, no way, no how
No matter what the path might contain
Whether water or fire, blessing or pain
But oh, my precious Lord, the grace you give
Strengthens and empowers and enables me to live
I'm going through, I will not turn back
There's nothing behind me but all kinds of lack
As long as I move forward you are by my side
Turning everything around for my good as in You I abide
If I choose to go back to nothing, I would lose you too
Then faith would turn to fear and I would displease you
So I choose you no matter where you lead
And I know you will always meet my every need

Only When

Oh Lord, the closer I get the more clearly I see
That there is not much of anything
that I can leave up to me
Use to there was so much that I thought I knew
But as time goes on it seems to change up my view
The more you reveal the more I definitely know
It is only by Your Spirit, that to me, you do show
There is nothing of me that can help me to walk
Nor anything that for you could help me to talk
Only when I see you as my full strength
Will I be able to continue and go the whole length
Only when I see you as the only way
Will I listen fervently to all that you say
Only when I give up all reasoning of my own
Will I clearly see what you've already shown
Only when I choose to give up any and all of the pain
Will you pour out upon me, the latter-day rain
Only when I choose to let go of all things in my past

Will I receive your healing love that
through eternity will last
Only when I see that all you want to take is the bad
Then I will not ever have to be lonely or sad
So I know I must trust in you for all, no matter what
And never depend on what I know or what I do not
The more of myself I give unto you
The more you take and make it like new
So the things that once bothered me, bothers me no more
And I am free now where once I use to keep score
So take all of me Lord and help me to flow
Then I'll be free in every area to live and to grow

The Spirit of Truth and the Spirit of Deception

When you witness, do some not ever seem to hear,
Especially family members that are so very near?
Yet other people can't seem to hear enough
They want more and more of God's special stuff
Those that won't listen are from the world my friend
So don't get so upset and think it's just the end
If you are from God only those from God will hear
And those that are of the world they will only jeer
This is how you will recognize and be able to know
Who has the Spirit of Truth or deception, as you go

I John 4:4-6 (Amplified)

Saved but…Don't Want to Hear It, Walk it, or Talk It

There are so many Lord that say they believe
And asked you into their heart as they did receive
Yet they do not walk by the commands in Your Word
And it seems their understanding is gradually blurred
If you show them that they are heading off track
Then they say you are judging them
and criticizing their lack
Those who truly live for you want to know all along
If something is not right and they are headed for wrong
In 1st John Your Word is very, very clear
Only those who obey it, are the ones that you keep near
Those who truly walk in God's presence
will not be able to keep
All the things that God has done in them, way down deep
It will be like fire shut up in your bones
And you'll have to tell someone about
it, even if it's to the stones
If you walk with God daily you can't keep it on a shelf

So if you don't want to hear about it
then, please, examine yourself
The enemy could be slowly leading you astray
By a deceiving spirit that he put in your way
So if you start taking notice of what's going on with you
And see you are growing colder and
don't know what to do
Repent and ask God to remove the
hindrances that are there
And He will gladly renew you and fresh fire He'll share

A Stronghold of Heaviness Is Broken

Oh my soul, why are you cast down again?
It is so grievous to me when it does begin
Each time did I think that I'd gotten rid of it
Then he would come back in, bit by bit
At this time, I can't even think
All that is around me does fade and blink
It seems that I'm all alone inside this place
And there is nothing at all that I am able to face
Even daily living becomes such a blur
And simple order disappears in the midst of the stir
At times it lifts its hand and lets me see
All of the undone things that should not be
Like a spear shot through my whole being
Does it pin me to the ground with what I am seeing
So quickly I try to do the things that I see
Then does this horrible thing come back down on me
Lord what is this thing that comes and goes
And has stolen order from me as it very well knows

As you show me this thing Lord that was also on my dad
It also tended to be heavy on him and make him very sad
This heaviness made him feel like he
failed and could not serve you
It kept him from fulfilling all that you put him here to do
I thank you Jesus you are my eternal defender
Into Your hands do I completely surrender
In the Name of Jesus, this stronghold is broken
Never can you return to me, for it has been spoken

Why Is My Life Draining Out?

Why Lord is the life inside me draining out?
So much so that I feel I'm in a drought
First I was so thirsty and so did I pray
Now am I past thirsty and do I now say
You and You alone Lord are all knowing
Please give me your wisdom by simply showing
There is some type of blockage that is in the way
And it seems to be growing more and more each day
You say it is not growing, it's been there all along
You've been uncovering it and that's
why it seems so strong
It is so very ugly and it is stealing my life
It has almost cut out my hope, just like a knife
This is one of the worst that I've come across
And it makes me feel like all is a loss
Like a ship, a vessel wrecked and dashed to pieces
The storm and all its fury seemingly never ceases
It literally feels that I'm right at death's door
And I have no other feelings anymore

Little one, there is a life inside you that I am taking out
It kept itself hid so well and now is very stout
You feel like you are dying because this
is the life that you have known
As I lead you from the death and all
its seeds that have been sown
The place I am taking you to you have not yet seen
Here death can never torment you
and your senses will be keen
So let this life of death drain out
And I will show you what real life is all about
"Don't look back at all the things that you have lost"
But look to me and go forward, and I
will exceedingly, overpay the cost
The death that is in you must die here along with its plan
You cannot take death and its curses to
the new and Promised Land
You feel so near death because I've called it to the top
It is time now that it is brought to a stop
Death has had his hand on you and
now it is the close of his season
He was not able to turn you from me,
no matter what his reason
You will see all things changing right before your very eyes
I'm also sending you my wisdom to make you very wise

To whom much is given, much is
required, you already know
You have asked for quite a lot, so just don't let me go
You are coming into a place of joy
that you have never known
But never get too lax, no matter what you are shown
Do not worry when and where you are to go
If you focus on me, you'll know
everything you need to know

The Seed and Root
of a Thought

Oh this tormenting battle that does rage within
Twisting and turning and pulling me thin
The enemy plants his seeds ever so small
Like that of an acorn that soon becomes tall
He covers it up and protects it until it does sprout
Then sends in thoughts, that will
strengthen it, until it grows out
Now he knows that there soon will be fruit
"Rotten actions of course as sure as the root"
So if I act ugly I must look down deep inside
And find that evil root that he tried to hide
"I must choose to replace it with thoughts that are right
So I will have good roots that grow
good fruit for the fight"
You will know (if) you are willing to take a look
Your actions and reactions will read like a book
Each action has a root from where it came
Good or bad, it will show you its name

There are people who will put on a show
They act like they do everything right, you know
They are not looking at their "thoughts
and intentions behind each act"
When these are the very things that will judge the fact
"It is your thoughts and intentions that the Lord does see
Not the outward appearance you've shown yourself to be"
You can never hide one thought or intent from His eyes
So why do you try to cover them by living in disguise
As you read this, please, let it uncover the veil
That will most assuredly, eventually cause you to fail
God has already purchased your
physical and spiritual wealth
Also along with your physical and spiritual health
So you say, "Why am I not walking in it then?"
I'm not purposely or knowingly living in sin
Wrong thoughts, intentions and
attitudes will keep you out
After years of battling against the enemy,
he eventually gets you to doubt
This is where some people grow faint or fall away
Thinking they messed up and entirely lost the way
Then the enemy comes in with
heaviness to break their spirit
Their hope and faith is then stolen,
as they no longer hear it

I pray you see and hear what is being said
So you do not end up spiritually dead
Jesus, in the wilderness, told Satan,
"In me you have no place"
At the onset of each thought and trial,
He gave him not a single space
We must do the same as each thought does try to come in
So we don't give Satan a place that will cause us to sin
We must examine our every action, attitude and intention
And determine by the Word if it's
of God or Satan's invention
We must ask God to help us get rid of any and every place
That we unknowingly gave the enemy
that might have hindered our race
Ask God then to completely fill you with His perfect love
So that every thought, intent and attitude
are then born from above

Don't Let Deception
Steal Your Faith

A test, yet at first, not seen as one
With the weight that feels like more than a ton
Still another test after all I have been through
But I know I must press on, endure and pursue
At times, during a trial, knowing
what to do is hid in a cloud
Confusion and doubt try to cover it
up and hide it like a shroud
Hoping if they can wait you out, your
confidence will deteriorate
Once confidence is broken, faith won't work,
which is what they want to obliterate
You must choose not to ever let go of God's hand
No matter how thick the confusion and
doubt, while you make your stand
If you hold that position you will eventually see
God's light breaking through that death
and destruction that tried to be

Deception once again has lost its long fight
Under the disguise of doubt and
confusion it sent in the night
But oh, how powerful the bright and morning star
No matter how long and dark that your nights are
Do not let deception deceive you along the way
Telling you that you don't have faith,
while he's draining it away
God gave every person a measure of faith and it is true
Never, ever, let deception cause you
to think faith's not in you
He may try to hide your faith from you
by covering it up for a time
But stand firm and do not accept it and
light will break forth and shine

Our Nation Is Covered

With intense compassion, our country feels the pain
Of all the precious loved ones that wrongly have been slain
But, let this be known, let it be said loud and clear
Let it be heard around the world by every single ear
God Himself has set us up as the head and not the tail
It is He who leads and guides us and we shall-not-fail
It's His compassion poured out through
us each time that we give
Reaching out to help other nations, let us always live
To those who choose to destroy and to violate
This Nation's kindness that God does initiate
That the heat of tragedy does only forge
A stronger weapon that shall cause you to disgorge
So no matter what kind of attack may take place
We are truly covered by God's mercy and His grace

Let Me Become One with You Lord

Lord let me be melted into you
Thoroughly enmeshed through and through
After the trash has been burned away
There'll be no weakness to pull me astray
Greater in strength as in you I become one
And the Holy Spirit seals us, never to be undone
Layer by layer is put through the fire
Burning what's dead and distorting God's desire
Hold me my Father, help me cling entirely to you
Let me not pull back but follow all the way through
At the end of each new trial I receive
A fresh new anointing that does conceive
And births within me a greater need
To please you more in word and deed

Never Alone

I accepted You Jesus into my heart
From this treasure I shall never depart
My Lord, my savior chooses to live in me
I chose to ask Him and He came quickly you see
Now I am never alone no matter where I go
My precious Lord is with me and this I always know
People come and people go, in and out of my life
But my Lord is with me always and
with Him there is no strife
He comforts and consoles me when I need His love
And sometimes a person is sent to
me from guidance up above
He heals me when I start to feel bad
He is the ultimate friend I've ever had
He supplies me with my every need
And I just continue to plant my seed
He talks to me and me with Him
Oh what a precious, precious gem
Loneliness is a word that I choose never to feel

How can I when Jesus is more—than—real
How in the universe can I ever be lonely
When I live with my Lord the One and only?

Rest in His Timing

His timing is perfect so why do we doubt
Why do we push, pull, scream and shout
Do we truly think we can move God's hand
So it's done on our time and not in His plan?
If we do then we have much to learn
And around that mountain again, we'll have to turn
It is He who created the earth and all that is
So perfect is the timing of all that is His
From sun and moon and tides of the ocean
To the world rotating on its axis in perfect motion
All our times are in His hands and He will let us know
When to do and what to do and when to let it go
We need only to be faithful to pray, seek and ask
While doing all for God's glory in each and every task
Then rest in His timing and let Him open the door
This will bring peace and He'll then give you more

I Gave All—What Will You Do?

My Father how do you bear the things you see
Murder, incest, rape, oppression and all that will be
There is nothing that can be hid from your view
It is all open and laid bare before you
Some ask why you don't stop it since you see
And why do you even allow it to be?
"It is not me allowing these things to be done
It is each one of you living under the sun
I have done all that needs to be done
I have given all by giving My Son
When I gave Him He became the door to all
Everything that you ever have need of, as you call
He overcame the enemy and gave you back the power
To walk on and over the enemy at any and every hour
If you don't pray, you should not complain
Through prayer is how you will regain
So you see, my child, I have done all I need to do
I can only do more as you let me act through you
You are my mouth, feet and hands

I wait on you to make a stand
So if you're tired of how things are going now
Act on My word in love and I will show you how"

Help People Understand the Way

Father so many people are angry and do not see
Please help them understand so they will not be
They want to blame you instead of
thanking you for what you've done
Help them see so they can go to
heaven by choosing Your Son
How horrendous and heart ripping it must be
That it goes against all that you wanted to see
Yes my child, a lot of people don't understand
This is not what I had planned
I gave My Son and He willingly paid the price for all
So if they accept Him as savior,
heaven will be their final call
I made a way for each one but each one must choose
It is by their choice that they win or will lose
I've made my choice to save them all
But some will reject me and they will fall
I love them so dearly that I gave up my Son
But I will not ever try to force not even one

Even though I've made a way for each
and every soul to be saved
There are those who will choose to stay on
the road where they've become enslaved
My Word says there is a way which seems right to a man
But the end of that way is death, this is not God's plan
I made hell for the devil and for people to shun
Yet people send their selves there
by rejecting Jesus, My Son
Don't choose hell, your ticket to heaven has been paid
It is so simple to accept the way that I have made

No Good-byes

If you're a child of God and it is time to go through death
There is absolutely no fear as you breathe your last breath
Death only has the right to take the flesh house we live in
But our soul and spirit returns unto God once again
That's it, that's all death can do
So don't let him torment you
A brand new body God will give
If for Him you do live
Who wants to keep a body ravaged by time and sin
Let Him give you an immortal body,
better than it's ever been
No aches no pains no sorrow no hardship
Only God's goodness and love as we all worship
So there is no need to say goodbye when that day is here
Just say, "I'll see you soon," and then
you hold that memory near
Yes there will be hurt from them not being at your side
But you will know they are safe and
sound as with Him they abide

All you have to do is finish the work
that God put you here to do
And then you will meet up with your
loved ones after you are through

Afterword

For everyone who wants their sins forgiven and washed away, for everyone caught up in the occult in any area and has been told there is no way out, for any soul that wants to make heaven their home instead of a burning hell full of nothing but eternal torment, please say this prayer with all of your heart, and you instantly become a child of the Most High God. There might be a battle, but God is on your side, and to be absent from the body is to be present with the Lord! In Jesus name I rebuke all fear and doubt of each soul reading this word and thank You Lord for sending warring angels to battle any and every hindrance to their salvation and deliverance.

A Sinner's Prayer to Receive Jesus as Savior

Dear Heavenly Father,

I come to you in the name of Jesus. Your Word says in John 6:37, "Those that come to me I will never reject." So I know that you will not reject me, and I thank you for it. You also said in Romans 10:13 that whosoever will call upon the name of the Lord shall be saved. I am calling on your name, so I know you have saved me now. You also said in Romans 10:9–10 that if I confess with my mouth the Lord Jesus and shall believe in my heart that God has raised him from the dead, I shall be saved. For with the heart man believeth unto righteousness, and with the mouth confession is made to salvation. I believe in my heart that Jesus Christ is the Son of God. I believe that He was raised from the dead for my justification. I confess Him now as my Lord, because your word says, "With the heart man believes unto righteousness," and I do believe with my heart. I have now become the righteousness of God in Christ (2 Corinthians 5:21), and I am saved! (King James or Amplified)

Thank you, Lord!

Now when you read this and confess it, write the date down in your Bible or somewhere. This is the day you were born again into the family of God, and now your true residence is heaven, and you seek God to find out what he put you here to do and get it done; then we get to spend eternity in heaven with an awesome, supernatural Father who is always creating new things to entertain and share with his children. Welcome to the family! Now find out who you are in Christ by reading the word and asking to be filled with the Holy Spirit (read in the book of Acts in the Bible), who is our teacher and friend. Find a good Bible teaching church that is not just a feel good church but will help you grow in the Word of God.